KOREAN COOKBOOK

70 Easy Recipes for Preparing Traditional Food from Korea

Maki Blanc

© **Copyright 2021 by Maki Blanc - All rights reserved.**

This document is geared towards providing exact and reliable information in regards to the topic and issue covered. The publication is sold with the idea that the publisher is not required to render accounting, officially permitted, or otherwise, qualified services. If advice is necessary, legal or professional, a practiced individual in the profession should be ordered.

- From a Declaration of Principles which was accepted and approved equally by a Committee of the American Bar Association and a Committee of Publishers and Associations.

It is not legal in any way to reproduce, duplicate, or transmit any part of this document in either electronic means or in printed format. Recording of this publication is strictly prohibited and any storage of this document is not allowed unless with written permission from the publisher. All rights reserved.

The information provided herein is stated to be truthful and consistent, in that any liability, in terms of inattention or otherwise, by any usage or abuse of any policies, processes, or directions contained within is the solitary and utter responsibility of the recipient reader. Under no circumstances will any legal responsibility or blame be held against the publisher for any reparation, damages, or monetary loss due to the information herein, either directly or indirectly.

Respective authors own all copyrights not held by the publisher.

The information herein is offered for informational purposes solely, and is universal as so. The presentation of the information is without contract or any type of guarantee assurance.

The trademarks that are used are without any consent, and the publication of the tradcmark is without permission or backing by the trademark owner. All trademarks and brands within this book are for clarifying purposes only and are the owned by the owners themselves, not affiliated with this document.

CONTENTS

INTRODUCTION..8

CHAPTER 1: KOREAN FOOD AT A GLANCE............10

1.1 History of Korean Cuisine...10

1.2 History of Traditional Korean Dishes 11

1.3 Health Benefits of Korean Food 12

1.4 Key Ingredients to Prepare Korean Food..........................13

CHAPTER 2: KOREAN APPETIZERS AND BREAKFAST RECIPES 14

2.1 Korean Street Toast...14

2.2 Korean Tofu with Spicy Korean Ketchup 15

2.3 Spicy Korean BBQ Chicken Pizza...................................16

2.4 Korean Corn Cheese 18

2.5 Cucumber Boats with Crab Salad 19

2.6 Korean BBQ Breakfast Tacos...20

2.7 Korean Style Sausage Stir Fry..22

2.8 Korean Vegetable Jeon 23

2.9 Gochujang Mayo Tuna Patties..24

2.10 Korean Egg Sandwich 26

2.11 Gyeran Bap Korean Rice with Egg.................................28

2.12 Korean Breakfast Kimchi Egg Skillet 29

2.13 Kimchi Mandu 30

2.14 Soy Garlic Fried Chicken 32

2.15 Korean Egg Roll (Gyeranmari) 34

2.16 Pan Fried Korean Hobak Jeon 36

CHAPTER 3: KOREAN LUNCH, SOUPS AND SALAD RECIPES 38

3.1 Noodle Fries 38

3.2 Korean Rice Cakes with Honey 39

3.3 Hotteok (Sweet Korean Pancakes) 40

3.4 Tteokbokki - Spicy Korean Rice Cakes 41

3.5 Korean Beef Bowl Meal 43

3.6 Pork Bulgogi Rice Bowl 44

3.7 Bibimbap (Korean Rice with Mixed Vegetables) 45

3.8 Korean BBQ Chickpeas 47

3.9 Korean Goguma Mattang 48

3.10 Korean Red Bean Mochi 49

3.11 Kangaroo Meat BBQ 50

3.12 Easy Korean Homemade Kimchi 51

3.13 Korean Style Popcorn Chicken 52

3.14 Korean Chicken Wings 54

3.15 Kimchi Buchimgae 57

3.16 Korean BBQ Beef Ribs 58

3.17 Sangchu Geotjeori 59

5

CHAPTER 4: KOREAN DINNER AND DESSERTS RECIPES 61

4.1 Chapssal Donuts 61

4.2 Bulgogi Beef Recipe 62

4.3 Sweet Rice Bundt Cake 63

4.4 Korean Fried Chicken 65

4.5 Korean Walnut Pastry 67

4.6 Makgeolli Ice Cream 68

4.7 Nut-Free Energy Balls 70

4.8 Korean Steak, Kimchi, and Cauliflower Rice Bowls 71

4.9 Chapssaltteok 72

4.10 Hodduk (Korean Sweet Pancakes) 73

4.11 Dalgona - Korean Sugar Sponge Candy 74

4.12 Bungeoppang with Filling 75

4.13 Korean Shaved Ice Dessert 76

4.14 Baram Tteok 77

4.15 Korean Coffee Brownies 78

4.16 Bingsu with Sweet Red Beans 79

4.17 Paleo Songpyeon 80

CHAPTER 5: VEGETARIAN KOREAN RECIPES 83

5.1 Vegan Bibimbap 83

5.2 Mushroom Hot Pot 85

5.3 Vegan Tteokbokki 86

5.4 Zucchini Pancakes 87

5.5 Braised Potatoes 88

5.6 Korean White Radish Kimchi 90

5.7 Mushroom Bulgogi Lettuce Wraps 91

5.8 Crunchy Gochujang Cauliflower 93

5.9 Korean Vegan Kimchi 94

5.10 Quick Korean Spicy Slaw Recipe 96

5.11 Watermelon Kimchi 97

5.12 Classic Korean Bibimbap 98

5.13 Korean Soft Tofu Stew 100

5.14 Eggplant Rolls 101

5.15 Korean Spicy Pickled Cabbage 103

5.16 Chilled Soy Milk Noodle Soup 104

5.17 Tofu Gimbap 105

5.18 Korean Street Toast 106

5.19 Korean Green Salad 108

5.20 Korean Salad with Sesame Dressing 109

CONCLUSION 110

Introduction

"Food is better for the citizens," says a five-character phrase in China. There is also a saying in South Korea that means "King Kong Mountain Food Culture." This demonstrates China's and South Korea's food value. People's food needs are increasing in combination with the advancement of technology and the enhancement of people's living standards. Food has developed into a culture rather than merely a means of satiating our hunger. People nowadays pay close attention to scenic locations and tend to frequent local food and snack establishments.

Korean cuisine is the one of the popular food in Korea, and thousands of Koreans living in other countries. Korea's culinary is diverse, interesting, and gaining international popularity, ranging from the intricate rituals of the Korean king's court food to the cuisine of port areas like Seoul and the major ports of South Korea and Busan. Korean cuisine is unique, with flavors and tastes derived from various ingredients such as soy sauce, canola paste, sesame oil, salt, garlic, spice, and, most notably, chili pepper, which brings out its unique spicy flavor. Korea, in reality, is the world's largest garlic user, surpassing Italy. Depending on the season, the food varies, but it is heavily reliant on pickled vegetables stored by fermentation.

All meals are cooked simultaneously at a Korean dining table, and table configurations differ depending on the main traditional dish. A pair of utensils and a spoon are usually used to eat all foods. A Korean meal's appearance is almost as critical as its taste. The number of main dishes (banchan) that follow the popular rice, broth, and kimchi is typical of Korean servings' names. Banchan meals are small in proportion and refilled when eaten, as they are meant to be done at each meal. Although the types and amount of banchans vary by location, the portions are always generous.

This book, "Korean Cookbook," consists of five chapters with a detailed introduction to Korean cuisine and its health benefits with delicious Korean recipes. Chapter 1 is about Korean cuisine, Korean cuisine history, and health benefits. Moreover, it will also give details about Korean spices and cooking techniques used in Korean restaurants. Chapter 2, 3, and 4 are recipe chapters with appetizers and breakfasts, snacks and lunch, dinner, and dessert recipes. Chapter 5 is about famous Korean dishes from vegetarian side. Read this book and give your meals a Korean touch with its unique flavors and cooking methods.

Chapter 1: Korean Food at a Glance

The numerous side dishes (banchan) eaten during dinners distinguish Korean cuisine from many other delicacies. The number of main dishes can vary from two to twelve, but most meals include at least one. When you dine at a Korean restaurant, you will be served with various side dishes in bowls prior to your main course. These can range from veggies to beef to fish cooked in a variety of ways. There are no different Korean cuisine courses as there are in Western cuisines since everything is consumed at the same moment.

Almost every Korean meal starts with rice. Noodles are sometimes substituted for rice, but for the most part, everyone consumes a bowl of rice with their meal. There are also several low-carb alternatives. Each individual will usually have their cup of soup as well. Main dishes and the side dish such as meat, fish, or tofu are all eaten family-style in the center of the table. A broad stew can be substituted for the main course and eaten family-style at the dinner.

1.1 History of Korean Cuisine

Korea's history lasted hundreds of years, beginning with the earliest recorded ceramics makers in 8,000 BC and continuing through the development of towns and empires from dispersed tribal settlements and nomadic savages to human civilization.

Tiny bands of hunter-gatherers, no more than a hundred family members, were the first inhabitants of the Korean peninsula, and they were possibly semi-nomadic in that they pursued the food sources. As the population grew, these groups became tribes, and some of them started to settle in places where there was sufficient food to sustain them. These newly settled tribes started to build remote communities and cultivate small-scale farming. The settlements arose in size as a few animals were domesticated.

In Korea, there are seasons, and in the autumn, all kinds of veggies and plants are accessible. Monks and nuns also devised a number of methods for preserving food and storing these nutritious fruits and vegetables for the winter.

1.2 History of Traditional Korean Dishes

The peninsula's environment has influenced Korean culture, climate (hot, moist seasons and bitterly harsh weather), similarity to Japan and China, and the Japanese occupation from 1920 to 1940. The arrival of chili peppers to Korea by Portuguese merchants in the 17th century had an influence on the culinary. Chili peppers were commonly used in the cooking of Korean cuisine by the 18th and 19th centuries.

Buddhism arrived in Korea from South Asia and was quickly adopted by the most influential kingdoms. With the teachings of Buddha, meat consumption was outlawed in much of the country, resulting in an increase in predominantly vegetarian food production. The several small vegetable dishes today known as namul recipes are thought to have originated that way.

Korean cuisine is not presented in a time-based format with a steak salad, an appetizer, and the main course served in that order. Rather, in a "space-based" layout, all of the food's products are arranged on a specific table at the same time. As a consequence, a Korean meal is a communal table that anyone enjoys together, rather than a single table set where each individual eats only what is put next to them. The Korean meals do not consist of passive consumption of food consumed one after the other, but rather of an "active" table where each person can choose whatever he or she prefers from a variety of dishes on the menu. These Korean meal features have culminated in a culinary tradition that is unlike anything else on the planet.

1.3 Health Benefits of Korean Food

Including broth at every dinner, which implies loading up on a comparatively low but desired food, is one of the practices that can help Koreans stay slim and safe. Every meal includes more than enough veggies, most notably in the shape of kimchi, which is a robustly flavored, fermented cabbage. In addition to phytonutrients and fiber, kimchi contains lactic acid bacteria and other "healthy" bacteria, which some experts believe may help strengthen immune defenses.

Capsaicin, a chemical that has been shown to strengthen blood vessels and improve metabolism, is abundant in Chili pepper. However, there is such a thing as much more of a positive thing: intense kimchi intake has been associated with an increased risk of pancreatic cancer, likely due to the salts and iodine it includes.

1.4 Key Ingredients to Prepare Korean Food

Several of the side dishes are marinated, steamed, or preserved, and many are hot, as Koreans have mastered the art of food preservation over hundreds of years. Kimchi, Korea's popular fiery cabbage, is made up of over 100 fresh veggies, including some that aren't hot. Many of the toppings are eaten cold or at ambient temperature, despite the fact that Korean stews and curries are presented hot (just about boiling).

Since Korea is a peninsula, Koreans consume a lot of fish, while meat has become increasingly common in the last fifty years or so. Korean cuisine's most popular spice and sauce components are:

- Ginger
- Scallions
- Sesame oil
- Soy sauce
- Garlic
- Chili pepper flakes (kochukaru)
- Soybean paste (doenjang)
- Chili pepper paste (gochujang)

Chapter 2: Korean Appetizers and Breakfast Recipes

2.1 Korean Street Toast

Cooking Time: 20 minutes

Serving Size: 2

Ingredients:
- 4 slices of ham
- Ketchup
- 4 large eggs
- 4 slices of bread
- 40g cheddar cheese (grated)
- Sea salt
- 100g cabbage (chopped)
- Butter
- Pepper
- 35g carrots (chopped)
- 1 spring onion (chopped)

Method:
1. Add a little salt and peppers and place the eggs in a dish.
2. Transfer to the beaten egg, the green onions, carrot, and vegetables.
3. Over medium heat, warm a deep fryer and drop the egg and vegetable mixture in.
4. Try to form a rectangle with the beaten egg.

5. Use a dishtowel to clean the deep fryer, add a bit more oil, and fry the bread.
6. For two slices of toast, add the cheese. On top of the egg, place the omelet and ham and put on some BBQ sauce while cooking the crust's bottom side.
7. With the leftover slice, repeat.

2.2 Korean Tofu with Spicy Korean Ketchup

Cooking Time: 20 minutes

Serving Size: 4

Ingredients:

Main

- Cooking oil
- 250g tofu

Spicy Korean Ketchup Sauce

- Toasted sesame seeds
- Green onions
- 1 teaspoon sesame oil
- 1 teaspoon minced garlic
- 3 tablespoon ketchup
- ½ tablespoon soy sauce
- ½ tablespoon honey
- 1.5 tablespoon gochujang

Method:

1. In a mixing bowl, blend the components for the spicy Korean tomato sauce.

2. Combine all of the ingredients in a large mixing bowl and set aside.
3. Use kitchen paper, dry the thinly sliced tofu.
4. Cook the tofu in a medium bowl until lightly browned on all sides. Place the tofu aside after removing it from the pan.
5. In a pan over moderately low heat, add in the hot ketchup mixture and mix for 10 seconds.
6. Toss the tofu back into the skillet. Sesame seeds and green onions are sprinkled on top.

2.3 Spicy Korean BBQ Chicken Pizza

Cooking Time: 50 minutes

Serving Size: 4

Ingredients:

Main

- Extra virgin olive oil
- coriander leaves
- 4 tortillas
- 2 cups pizza cheese
- BBQ sauce
- 120g chicken thigh fillet
- ½ purple onion (sliced)
- 150g (sliced) pineapple pieces

Marinades

- ½ teaspoon raw sugar
- Ground black pepper
- 2 teaspoon Korean chili paste

- ¼ teaspoon (minced) ginger
- ½ teaspoon Korean chili flakes (gochugaru)
- 1 teaspoon of rice wine
- ½ teaspoon (minced) garlic
- ½ teaspoon soy sauce

Method:
1. Marinate the meat in the spice mix in the refrigerator for thirty minutes.
2. Cook the chicken until ready.
3. Placc the pizza dough in the oven and bake it for fifteen minutes at 410F.
4. On the tortilla bottom, spread the cheese around and insert some red onions and slices of pineapple.
5. Put the chicken pieces and the green leaves of your selection on the bottom.
6. Position the pizza on the base of the sheet pan and prepare until the cheese is melted.

2.4 Korean Corn Cheese

Cooking Time: 15 minutes
Serving Size: 6

Ingredients:

- 1 cup mozzarella cheese
- 2 green scallions
- 2 tablespoon white granulated sugar
- Salt and pepper
- 2 cans kernel corn
- 6 tablespoon mayonnaise
- ¼ cup unsalted butter

Method:

1. Combine corn, cream, mayo, and honey in a big cast iron skillet.
2. Preheat the skillet over medium heat. Season with salt and pepper and toss to combine.
3. Spray the layer with cheese until the combination is bubbling and sweet.
4. Place pan in the oven to end in the microwave.
5. Preheat the oven to a low broil temperature.
6. Allow 3-5 minutes for the cheese to broil.
7. Remove from the oven and top with spring onions.

2.5 Cucumber Boats with Crab Salad

Cooking Time: 10 minutes

Serving Size: 4

Ingredients:

- Fine sea salt to taste
- ground black pepper to taste
- 2 cucumber (rinsed)
- 3 tablespoon mayonnaise
- 25g onion (diced)
- 60g crab stick (diced)
- 25g yellow capsicums (diced)
- 25g red capsicums (diced)

Method:
1. Remove half the length of the cucumber.
2. Then use a small spoon to shape a boat and cut out the cucumber's seeds.
3. In a mixing bowl, place the rest of the ingredients and combine them well.
4. Split the mixture of crab salad equally and put it on the cucumber vessels. Serve immediately.

2.6 Korean BBQ Breakfast Tacos

Cooking Time: 3 hours 35 minutes

Serving Size: 6

Ingredients:

Bulgogi

- 6 garlic cloves (smashed)
- ½ cup (packed) light brown sugar
- ½ teaspoon (crushed) red pepper flakes
- 3 pounds boneless short ribs (sliced)
- ¾ cup low-sodium soy sauce
- 6 scallions (sliced)
- 2 teaspoons (grated) ginger
- ½ cup of fish sauce
- 2 tablespoons sesame oil

Slaw

- 2 tablespoons Sriracha
- ⅓ cup olive oil
- 3 cups (shredded) napa cabbage
- 2 tablespoons low-sodium soy sauce
- 2 tablespoons fish sauce
- ½ cup (sliced) daikon
- 6 scallions (sliced)
- 2 limes (juiced)
- ½ cup (sliced) carrots
- ¼ cup (chopped) fresh cilantro

Tacos

- 8 large eggs
- 4 scallions (sliced)
- 12 small tortillas
- 2 garlic cloves (minced)

- 1 tablespoon olive oil

Method:

1. Put the soy sauce, oyster sauce, cinnamon, sesame oil, cloves, fresh basil, seasoning, and red pepper in a blender.
2. With the chopped short ribs, process until well combined and pour into a wide cup.
3. Cover and refrigerate for at least four hours or overnight with plastic wrap.
4. Set a gas stove kettle grill over medium temperature to cook the bulgogi.
5. Toss the onions, carrots, daikon, cilantro, and scallions with each other in a large bowl.
6. Mix the lemon zest, soy sauce, Sriracha, fish sauce, and olive oil in a shallow bowl.
7. Place the vegetables over and mix until well balanced. Set aside.
8. Insert the olive oil, green onions, and garlic. Cook for a minute, then add the white rice and mix.
9. Heat the tortillas in a clean skillet to assemble the tacos. Split the poached eggs between all the bulgogi, tortillas, and slaw.

2.7 Korean Style Sausage Stir Fry

Cooking Time: 10 minutes

Serving Size: 4

Ingredients:

Main

- 40g onion (julienned)
- Some cooking oil
- 70g bell peppers (julienned)
- 200g Korean style Vienna sausage

Sauce

- ½ tablespoon raw sugar
- ½ tablespoon soy sauce
- 2 tablespoon tomato sauce

Method:

1. Add enough cooking oil to a hot skillet.
2. Cook the sausage over moderate flame.
3. Mix till the sausage is quarter cooked.
4. Add the bell peppers and onions.
5. Mix and heat until they are softened.
6. Turn the heat down to moderate flame.
7. Put in the sauce and blend with the remaining ingredients.
8. Take the skillet from the heat.
9. Represent it with fried rice and other main dishes from Korea.

2.8 Korean Vegetable Jeon

Cooking Time: 30 minutes

Serving Size: 20 pancakes

Ingredients:
Jeon Vegetable Pancakes

- vegetable oil
- sesame oil
- 2 cup zucchini
- 1 teaspoon salt
- ¼ teaspoon black pepper
- 1 large egg (beaten)
- ¾ cup of water
- 1 ½ cup carrots (grated)
- ¾ cup orange pepper (diced)
- 2 cup all-purpose flour
- 2 cup yellow potatoes (grated)
- ¾ cup green onions (diced)

Spicy Soy Dipping Sauce

- 2 cloves garlic (diced)
- 1 green jalapeno pepper
- 3 tablespoon soy sauce
- 1 tablespoon onion (chopped)
- 2 tablespoon rice vinegar

Method:
1. Put all the vegetables in a big bowl.

2. When well dispersed, stir flour into veggies.
3. Insert the egg and ¾ cup of water, then stir.
4. Add the remaining ¼ cup of water if the batter is very dry.
5. Stir in the pepper and salt and mix well.
6. In a skillet, heat ½ tablespoons of olive oil or cooking oil.
7. Switch the pancake and drizzle a tiny amount of sesame oil.
8. To absorb the excess liquid, remove the pancake from the skillet and position it on a table covered with a clean cloth.
9. Add extra sunflower oil or vegetable oil as required.

2.9 Gochujang Mayo Tuna Patties

Cooking Time: 16 minutes

Serving Size: 10

Ingredients:

Main

- 1 cup panko
- Some cooking oil
- 185g canned tuna (drained)
- 1 teaspoon gochujang
- Ground black pepper
- ¼ teaspoon fine sea salt
- 2 tablespoon mayonnaise
- 20g green bell peppers (chopped)

- 2 teaspoon all-purpose flour
- 2 large eggs (beaten)
- 20g green onion (chopped)
- 20g red bell pepper (chopped)
- 45g onion (chopped)

Gochujang Mayo Dipping Sauce

- ¼ cup mayonnaise
- 2 teaspoon Korean chili paste (gochujang)

Soy Dipping Sauce

- 1 tablespoon rice wine vinegar
- 2 teaspoon sugar
- 1 tablespoon water
- 1 tablespoon soy sauce

Method:

1. Prepare your dipping sauce by stirring all components in a bowl and reserve.
2. In a small cup, whisk together the mayonnaise and gochujang.
3. In a mixing bowl, mix the eggs, canned tuna, green onion, cabbage, gochujang mayo sauce, bell peppers, flour, salt, and ½ cup panko breadcrumbs.
4. Form into tiny balls of the solution.
5. Gently put them on panko and turn around to cover.
6. Compress the balls softly with your palms into patties.
7. Over moderately low heat, heat the oil in a pan.

8. Put the tuna patties softly in the pan and seal with the lid and continue cooking.
9. Place the 356 F air fryer and bake for 10 minutes.
10. Serve hot with your selection of dipping sauce.

2.10 Korean Egg Sandwich

Cooking Time: 50 minutes

Serving Size: 1

Ingredients:

- ¼ cup asparagus (sliced)
- virgin coconut oil
- 5 large eggs
- ¼ cup green onion (chopped)
- ¼ cup shitake mushrooms (sliced)
- ¼ cup carrot (chopped)
- ¼ cup yellow onion (chopped)
- ¼ teaspoon kosher salt
- ¼ teaspoon white vinegar
- ¼ teaspoon black pepper
- 1 tablespoon whole milk

Method:

1. In a mixing saucepan, whisk the salt, eggs, spice, milk, and cider until well mixed and smooth.
2. In a clean pan, pour the beaten eggs through a filter paper or fine mesh strainer.
3. Add the veggies and a dash of salt and peppers when the oil begins to shimmer.

4. Remove from heat and put on a plate lined with a clean cloth.
5. When cool enough to handle the veggies, spill them into the beaten egg, and blend vigorously with a spoon to combine.
6. Heat 1 teaspoon of olive oil in the pan using the same 12-inch nonstick skillet, and move it around to cover the dish.
7. Add ¼ of the beaten egg over medium-low heat and rotate the skillet gently to spread the eggs and vegetables evenly.
8. Roll the eggs softly or fold them over.
9. To the pan's exposed side, add half the remaining beaten egg and gently swirl it around to balance it out.
10. Roll up the whole egg roll and then let it heat in the skillet for another two minutes.
11. Take the egg roll from the bowl and let it sit for a couple of minutes on a baking sheet.

2.11 Gyeran Bap Korean Rice with Egg

Cooking Time: 10 minutes
Serving Size: 1

Ingredients:

- Roasted sesame seeds
- Fresh scallions diced
- 1 tablespoon soy sauce
- 1 tablespoon sesame oil
- 1 tablespoon vegetable oil
- 2 cups cooked rice
- 1 large egg

Method:

1. Add the oil to a medium nonstick skillet over medium heat.
2. Crack an egg into the bowl with care.
3. Turn the heat down and remove the cap.
4. Sprinkle the sesame oil and soy sauce over the boiled rice and cover with the eggs in a small bowl or cup.
5. Scatter some finely diced green onion on top.

2.12 Korean Breakfast Kimchi Egg Skillet

Cooking Time: 25 minutes

Serving Size: 2

Ingredients:

- 1 teaspoon lemon juice
- 1 green onion
- ½ teaspoon chili garlic sauce
- 2 teaspoons mayonnaise
- ½ cup oyster mushrooms
- ½ cup kimchi
- ½ teaspoon tamari
- 1 teaspoon ginger
- 1 teaspoon olive oil

Method:

1. In a medium-sized skillet, heat the oil. Add the ginger, as well as the sliced mushrooms.
2. Heat for several minutes or until the mushrooms are golden brown.
3. Cook for a few minutes after adding the kimchi.
4. In the mix, make four nests and break four eggs, one through each nest.
5. Cook over medium heat until the eggs are cooked through.
6. Combine tamari, masala Olek, mayonnaise, and lime juice in a shallow saucepan. Blend until fully smooth.
7. Serve the eggs with a drizzle of sauce and a sprinkling of green onions.

2.13 Kimchi Mandu

Cooking Time: 1 hour 10 minutes
Serving Size: 25 dumplings

Ingredients:

Dumpling Skin

- Some water
- 25 dumpling wrappers (large)

Dumpling Fillings

- ½ teaspoon (minced) garlic
- Ground black peppers
- 1½ cups kimchi (chopped)
- 1 teaspoon fine sea salt
- 1 teaspoon sesame oil
- 250g tofu (minced)
- 200g mung bean sprouts (chopped)
- 10g garlic chives (chopped)
- ½ onion (chopped)
- 1 egg
- 130g (minced) pork

Others

- ¼ cup of water
- Some cooking oil

Method:

1. In a blending pan, mix and combine the filling materials.
2. Put a dumpling wrap on your hand and transfer it to the middle of the wrapper with the filling.
3. Enclose the wrapper, then position it on a non-stick level surface.

4. As per your choice, cook mandu. Transfer some cooking oil to a well-heated dish.
5. Place several mandu and fry until the mandu base is nicely browned.
6. Turn the heat down to medium or moderate.
7. This will guarantee that the meat is tender completely without burns.
8. Place other non-stick items on a container and place the mandu inside it.
9. Position the steamer over running hot water and cook the mandu over moderately low heat for 20 minutes.
10. With Korean dumpling sauces, put the mandu in a bowl.

2.14 Soy Garlic Fried Chicken

Cooking Time: 40 minutes

Serving Size: 6

Ingredients:
Chicken and Seasonings

- ¼ teaspoon ginger powder
- Ground black pepper
- 900g chicken thigh fillets
- 1 teaspoon garlic powder
- 1 teaspoon fine sea salt
- 1 teaspoon onion powder
- 2 tablespoon rice wine

Other

- cooking oil
- 1.5 cups of corn starch

Soy Garlic Sauce

- 2 tablespoon water
- 2 green onions (optional)
- ¼ cups soy sauce
- Ground black pepper
- 3 dried chilies (optional)
- ½ tablespoon (minced) garlic
- 2 tablespoon brown sugar
- 2 tablespoon rice wine
- ½ tablespoon (minced) ginger

- 2 tablespoon honey

Slurry

- 2 teaspoon water
- 2 teaspoon corn starch

Garnish

- green onions (sliced)
- toasted sesame seeds

Method:

1. Put the minced chicken in a wide bowl and whisk in the rice wine, garlic powder, onion, seasoning powder, salt, and pepper.
2. In a wide bowl, put the corn starch in it. In the corn starch, add the seasoned chicken parts and cover them uniformly.
3. Add a reasonable amount of oil to a large skillet.
4. Add additional chicken thoroughly and fry it until it cooks.
5. Once the oil temperature hits 347 F, pan-fries the chicken once again.
6. Fry them until they are crispy and translucent in the batter.
7. Mix all the sauce ingredients in a small saucepan. Carry it to a boil over medium-high heat, stirring regularly.
8. Merge and mix the slurry components in a small pan.
9. Turn off the heat and cool longer than 5 minutes until the mixture thickens.
10. On the rimmed baking sheet, position the double-fried chicken, carefully braise the chicken with the sauces using a cooking brush.

11. Garnish with sesame seeds and spring onions until all the chicken is covered with the sauce. Serve hot.

2.15 Korean Egg Roll (Gyeranmari)

Cooking Time: 50 minutes

Serving Size: 1

Ingredients:

- ¼ cup asparagus (sliced)
- virgin coconut oil
- 5 large eggs
- ¼ cup green onion (chopped)
- ¼ cup shitake mushrooms (sliced)
- ¼ cup carrot (chopped)
- ¼ cup yellow onion (chopped)
- ¼ teaspoon kosher salt
- ¼ teaspoon white vinegar
- ¼ teaspoon black pepper
- 1 tablespoon whole milk

Method:

1. In a mixing saucepan, whisk the salt, eggs, spice, milk, and cider until well mixed and smooth.
2. In a clean pan, pour the beaten eggs through a filter paper or fine mesh strainer.
3. For a 12-inch small saucepan, add 1 teaspoon of olive oil.
4. Add the veggies and a dash of salt and peppers when the oil begins to shimmer.

5. Remove from heat and put on a plate lined with a clean cloth.
6. When cool enough to handle the veggies, spill them into the beaten egg, and blend vigorously with a spoon to combine.
7. Heat 1 teaspoon of olive oil in the pan using the same 12-inch nonstick skillet, and move it around to cover the dish.
8. Add ¼ of the beaten egg over medium-low heat and rotate the skillet gently to spread the eggs and vegetables evenly.
9. Let the mixture cook for 3-4 minutes until the eggs are ready to set and just a little fluid is left in the pot.
10. Take it from one hand and roll the eggs softly or fold them over.
11. To the pan's exposed side, add half the remaining beaten egg and gently swirl it around to balance it out.
12. Roll up the whole egg roll and then let it heat in the skillet for another two minutes.
13. Cut the egg roll into 2-inch parts.

2.16 Pan Fried Korean Hobak Jeon

Cooking Time: 20 minutes

Serving Size: 4

Ingredients:

- ¾ teaspoon fine sea salt (divided)

- Some cooking oil
- 1 Korean zucchini
- 2 eggs (beaten)
- 3 tablespoon all-purpose flour

Method:
1. Place the diced zucchini on a level surface. Uniformly spray salt across the zucchini.
2. Clean any extra liquid with paper towels from the zucchini softly.
3. In a freezer bag, put the flour and leftover salt and insert the zucchini.
4. Move the bag with one side while gripping the open end firmly, ensuring that the zucchini is uniformly covered.
5. One by one, remove the zucchini from the packet, shake thoroughly off the excess flour, and dip it into a cup of the beaten egg.
6. Coat all sides of the zucchini in clusters with the egg, over moderate to low heat, heat a pan.
7. Insert some olive oil once warmed and scatter well. Position the zucchini carefully and prepare both sides until slightly golden brown.
8. To prevent overheating, it is essential to cook the zucchini over moderate to moderately low heat.
9. Cooking on both ends will take about 3-4 minutes, but it will depend on your zucchini width.
10. Switch them around halfway over. Perhaps you need to prepare them in groups.
11. Transfer to a dish: offer fried rice, Korean pancake sauce, and other main dishes from Korea.

Chapter 3: Korean Lunch, Soups and Salad Recipes

3.1 Noodle Fries

Cooking Time: 15 minutes

Serving Size: 2

Ingredients:

- ½ tablespoon (toasted) sesame seeds
- Some vegetable oil
- 1 Nuclear fire noodle cup
- 4 sheets seasoned seaweed (crushed)
- 300g French fries (frozen)

Method:

1. Following the package instructions, shallow fry the French fries.
2. With your cooking style, you might need a microwave or air fryer.
3. Meanwhile, over medium-high heat, heat some water in a different pot.
4. Add the noodles and simmer for 50 seconds until the water is quickly boiling.
5. Move them into the bowl and mix once the noodles become crispy.
6. Combine the flake sauce that came with the noodles.
7. Add the spicy seasoning that came with the noodles as well.

8. To coat, flip softly. Add extra seasoning seaweed and sesame seeds to garnish.

9. Shift into the noodle bowl. You can top it off with some more hot sauce.

3.2 Korean Rice Cakes with Honey

Cooking Time: 10 minutes

Serving Size: 1

Ingredients:

- 2 tablespoon honey
- Sesame seeds, for garnish
- ½ tablespoon butter
- 100-gram Korean rice cakes

Method:

1. Just use frozen rice cakes, soak them in hot water for 20-30 minutes, or till softened.
2. Make a separation between the rice cakes.
3. Preheat a frying pan on medium-low heat.
4. Add the butter and stir until it is completely melted.
5. Cook for around 4-5 minutes, just until the rice cakes are light brownish and crispy from the outside.
6. Serve warm, drizzled with sugar, and topped with sesame seeds.

3.3 Hotteok (Sweet Korean Pancakes)

Cooking Time: 3 hours 30 minutes
Serving Size: 10 pancakes

Ingredients:
For Dough
- ¾ teaspoon salt
- 1 cup sweet rice flour
- 1 teaspoon instant dry yeast
- 1 cup all-purpose flour
- 6 tablespoon water

Yeast Solution
- 1 teaspoon sugar
- ¾ cup of water

For Stuffing
- ½ teaspoon cinnamon powder
- ¼ cup (chopped) walnuts
- ½ cup (unbleached) sugar

Frying
- 7 tablespoon vegetable oil for frying

Method:
1. In a ¾ cup of warm boiling water, add a small teaspoon of sugar and 1 teaspoon of dry yeast.
2. Combine well while the yeast is bubbly.
3. Mix the yeast and sugar water with the flour mix and extra water.
4. Let the dough come to room temperature for 3 hours.

5. Mix the sugar, spices, and sliced walnuts to prepare the stuffing.
6. Heat approximately 3 tablespoons or more oil in the pan over medium-high heat when the dough is prepared.
7. Take some dough in your palm about the small size and stretch it out with your palms until it is slightly larger than your hand.
8. Into the dough's middle, put two teaspoons of the sugar mixture and close the hotteok, creating a little round shape.
9. Fry the pancake for 4 minutes in medium-hot oil until the edges begin to brown.

3.4 Tteokbokki - Spicy Korean Rice Cakes

Cooking Time: 20 minutes

Serving Size: 2

Ingredients:

Main

- 60g onion (sliced)
- 350g Korean rice cakes (separated)
- 2 cups Korean soup stock
- 150g Korean fish cakes

Tteokbokki Sauce

- 1 teaspoon (minced) garlic
- 1 teaspoon gochugaru
- 3 tablespoon gochujang (Korean chili paste)
- 1 tablespoon soy sauce

- 1½ tablespoon raw sugar

Garnish
- 1 stalk green onion (chopped)
- 1 teaspoon sesame oil
- 1 teaspoon toasted sesame seeds

Method:
1. When your rice cakes are tender, steam them for ten minutes in hot water.
2. In a deep saucepan over medium heat, heat the broth stock and absorb the tteokbokki liquid by mixing with a spoon.
3. Insert the fish cakes, rice cakes, and onions when the seasoned stock is heating.
4. Once the rice cakes are cooked thoroughly, boil them for another three to five minutes.
5. Then simmer it over medium heat for a further two to four minutes to thicken the sauce and enhance its flavor.
6. Stir in the sesame seed, the sesame oil, and the spring onions and stir rapidly.
7. Serve it hot.

3.5 Korean Beef Bowl Meal

Cooking Time: 25 minutes
Serving Size: 4

Ingredients:
- 4 cups hot cooked brown rice
- 1 tablespoon sesame seeds
- ¼ teaspoon red pepper
- 6 green onions
- 1 pound lean ground beef
- ½ cup soy sauce
- ⅓ cup light brown sugar
- 1 tablespoon ginger
- 2 teaspoons scsame oil
- 5 cloves garlic

Method:
1. In a medium saucepan, heat the oil over moderate flame.
2. Cook, mixing and crumbling the beef into tiny chunks until it is browned around 5 - 8 minutes. Remove any excess oil.
3. Stir in the garlic, onion, and sesame oil for around two minutes, or until fragrant.
4. Combine the soy sauce, coconut milk, and red pepper in a mixing bowl.
5. Cook for about 7 minutes, or when some of the sauce has absorbed into the meat.
6. Serve the beef with leftover spring onions and sesame seeds on top of hot cooked rice.

3.6 Pork Bulgogi Rice Bowl

Cooking Time: 50 minutes
Serving Size: 4

Ingredients:

Main

- 170g medium onion (julienned)
- Some cooking oil
- 1 tablespoon (toasted) sesame seeds
- 30g green onion (chopped)
- 600g pork shoulder

Marinade

- 3 tablespoon gochujang
- 3 tablespoon soy sauce
- 1 tablespoon garlic
- 1 tablespoon ginger
- 3 tablespoon honey
- 2 tablespoon gochugaru
- ¼ teaspoon ground black pepper
- 100g red apple
- 50g brown onion
- 2 tablespoon rice wine

Rice Bowl Serving Suggestions

- 10 leaves Lettuce (sliced)
- 10 leaves Korean perilla (sliced)
- Steamed rice
- 1 English cucumber (sliced)

Method:

1. For at least thirty minutes, marinate the meat in the gravy.

2. Place the marinated meat over medium-high heat in a well-heated skillet or pan until the meat is about seventy percent cooked (about 10 to 15 minutes).
3. Insert the onion and continue cooking until the meat is fully cooked.
4. Add spring onions and sesame seeds to garnish.
5. Serve the meat using steamed rice, clean lettuce, and Korean crispy dipping sauce.

3.7 Bibimbap (Korean Rice with Mixed Vegetables)

Cooking Time: 70 minutes

Serving Size: 4

Ingredients:

- Fried egg, (optional)
- Gochujang (red pepper paste)
- 2 cups of Korean rice
- 2 teaspoons salt (divided)
- ½ pound meat (optional)
- 1 zucchini (sliced)
- 2 tablespoons sesame oil (divided)
- 1 large cucumber (sliced)
- 1 ½ cups bean sprouts
- 2 carrots (julienned)
- 4 shiitake mushrooms
- 1 ½ cups spinach
- Dash of sesame seeds

Method:

1. Collect ingredients.
2. On the stove, prepare rice.
3. Then, offer the cucumber strip a ten minutes saltwater soak.
4. In saltwater, add cucumber pieces.
5. Then, put two teaspoons of sesame oil, 1 dash of salt, and a splash of sesame seeds into the spinach.
6. Spinach gets flavored with sesame seed, pepper, and sesame oil.
7. Use two tablespoons of sesame oil and a dash of sesame seeds to season the bean sprouts.
8. After that, you will have to sauté the carrots with a sprinkle of salt.
9. Next, give a touch of salt to the mushrooms.
10. Then in a large mixing bowl, place the rice and organize the veggies on it.
11. Beef, eggs, or even both can be positioned in the center if required.

3.8 Korean BBQ Chickpeas

Cooking Time: 50 minutes

Serving Size: 3

Ingredients:

- ¼ teaspoon garlic powder
- ¼ teaspoon onion powder
- 1 canned chickpea (rinsed)
- ¼ teaspoon fine sea salt
- ¼ teaspoon ginger powder
- 2 teaspoon olive oil
- 1 teaspoon soy sauce
- 1 teaspoon Korean chili flakes
- 2 teaspoon brown sugar

Method:

1. Shift well-drained chickpeas to an air-fryer bowl to ensure that they do not mix.
2. Fry them for five minutes at 212 F.
3. In a mixing bowl, pass the chickpeas, insert the olive oil and cover softly.
4. Move the chickpeas directly to the basket of the air fryer and scatter well.
5. Switch the temperature of the air fryer to 347F and cook the chickpeas for fifteen minutes in total.
6. Move the basket about halfway this time, though, even for baking.
7. Mix and shake the additional ingredients in a small cup, including brown sugar, Korean chili flakes, soy sauce, cinnamon, spice powder, garlic powder, and onion powder.
8. Switch the air fryer off if the chickpeas are done.
9. Move the seasoned chickpeas away to the air fryer's basket and scatter well so that they do not overlap.

10. Return the basket to the air fryer. In a cooled air fryer, fry the chickpeas for 30 minutes.
11. You can serve them as a side dish in your salad.

3.9 Korean Goguma Mattang

Cooking Time: 45 minutes

Serving Size: 4

Ingredients:
- 3 tablespoon raw sugar
- 1 tablespoon cooking oil
- 500g sweet potato
- Caramel sauce
- Some cooking
- Some nuts (crushed)

Method:
1. Clean the sweet potato, slice, and chop the surface into small pieces.
2. Rinse them for thirty minutes in cold water to eliminate the starch.
3. Take the water away and completely scrub the water with paper towels from the potatoes.
4. In a big kettle, add the frying oil and warm it up until it reaches 356 F.
5. Add the potatoes and simmer until they are fully cooked.
6. To drain away from the natural oils, take out the frying sweet potatoes and put them on some paper towels.

7. Heat it over medium-high heat until it melts the sugar, lowering the temperature to low rapidly.
8. In the bowl, add the potatoes and combine well for 2 minutes with the sauce.
9. To cool it down for five minutes, transfer the sweet potatoes to non-stick baking parchment. Immediately serve.

3.10 Korean Red Bean Mochi

Cooking Time: 24 minutes

Serving Size: 6

Ingredients:

- ¾ cup (sweetened) red bean paste (shape round)
- 3 tablespoon corn starch
- ¾ cup sweet rice flour
- A pinch fine sea salt
- ½ cup of water
- ¼ cup castor sugar

Method:
1. In a microwave-proof medium bowl, mix the sweet rice flour, salt, and sugar.
2. Fill a bowl with cling wrap, leaving a slight opening to escape from the steam. Put the bowl in an oven and heat it for around 1 minute.
3. Put the cup, covering again in the microwave, and heat it for another two minutes.
4. From the microwave, take the bowl.
5. Spread the corn starch gently on the surface.

6. Detach the mochi paste from the mixture carefully and put it on the board. Then, break the roll into six bits using a scraper.
7. Deflate softly and expand the dough on your hand, and position the red bean paste balls in the center.
8. By collecting the edges of the dough, cover the rice cake.
9. With the rest of the ingredients, replicate this step. Serve at ambient temperature.

3.11 Kangaroo Meat BBQ

Cooking Time: 8 hours 50 minutes

Serving Size: 3

Ingredients:

- 5 leaves dried bay
- 500g kangaroo rump steak (sliced)
- A dash of sesame oil

Marinade Sauce

- 5g (minced) ginger
- 10 whole black peppers
- 4 ½ tablespoon soy sauce
- 60g grated apple
- 1 tablespoon (minced) garlic
- 2 tablespoon dark brown sugar
- 40g grated onion
- 2 tablespoon rice wine

Method:

1. In ice water, wash the meat and try to clean the water lightly with paper towels.
2. Put the meat in a sealing bag, add the sauces, and mix it thoroughly with the meat.
3. Place the meat on the edge of the bay leaves and close the lid. Shift it and marinate it overnight in the refrigerator.
4. While cooking, take the meat out for 30 minutes and add a teaspoon of sesame oil and mix well.
5. Cook your meat on BBQ. Serve hot.

3.12 Easy Korean Homemade Kimchi

Cooking Time: 2 hours

Serving Size: 1

Ingredients:

For the Cabbage

- ½ cup sea salt
- 1 cup water
- 5 pounds napa cabbage

Seasonings For Kimchi

- ½ cup red pepper powder
- 1 bundle green onions
- 1 bulb garlic
- ¼ cup water
- ½ medium sweet onion

Method:

1. In a big mixing bowl, position the cabbage.

2. Spillover cabbage and toss with your hands to combine.
3. In the meanwhile, make a puree with the onions and cloves and ¼ cup sugar.
4. Combine in a medium mixing bowl with red pepper mixture and spring onions.
5. Rinse the cabbage until it has wilted to remove the majority of the saltwater.
6. Position the prepared kimchi in a big mason jar and push down the cabbage with your fist to compact it all into the jar.
7. Cover the Mason jar tightly and set aside at ambient temperature overnight.

3.13 Korean Style Popcorn Chicken

Cooking Time: 1 hour 5 minutes

Serving Size: 3

Ingredients:

Main

- 1 cup potato starch
- Some cooking oil
- 500g chicken thigh fillets
- ½ teaspoon fine sea salt
- ¼ teaspoon ground black pepper
- 150g Korean rice cake
- 2 teaspoon ginger powder
- 1 tablespoon rice wine

Sauce

- 2 teaspoon sesame oil
- ½ teaspoon (minced) garlic
- 5 tablespoon tomato sauce
- 2 tablespoon dark brown sugar
- 1 tablespoon soy sauce
- 1½ tablespoon gochujang
- 2 tablespoon honey

Optional
- (Crushed) nuts or seeds
- (Chopped) green onion

Method:
1. Set the pieces of chicken in a large bowl.
2. Balance well with rice wine, spice powder, salt, and pepper.
3. Close with the plastic wrap and marinate the chicken in the refrigerator for 30 minutes.
4. Cover each chicken part entirely with the starch powder.
5. In a large sauté pan, pour some olive oil and cook till it reaches 347F.
6. Fry the rice cakes until the outer layer becomes crispy.
7. Pounded chicken pieces are deep-fried in groups until crispy and heated through.
8. To absorb any natural oils, bring them out and toss them aside on paper towels.
9. For the leftover chicken, repeat this.
10. Twice fry them just one to two minutes to make the chicken creamier and set aside.

11. In a hot pan, pour the sauce.
12. Insert the crispy chicken and rice cakes and cover them rapidly and evenly with the gravy.
13. Garnish with your selection of toppings. Serve hot.

3.14 Korean Chicken Wings

Cooking Time: 25 minutes

Serving Size: 4

Ingredients:

Chicken and Base Seasonings

- ¼ teaspoon ginger powder
- Ground black peppers
- 900g chicken wings
- 1 teaspoon garlic powder
- 1 teaspoon fine sea salt
- 2 tablespoon rice wine
- 1 teaspoon onion powder

Soy Garlic Sauce

- 2 teaspoon corn starch
- 2 teaspoon water
- 3 tablespoon soy sauce
- 30g green onions
- 3 (dried) chilies (optional)
- Ground black peppers
- 2 tablespoon water

- 2 tablespoon honey
- 2 tablespoon rice wine
- 2 tablespoon brown sugar

Sweet and Spicy Sauce

- 1 tablespoon (minced) garlic
- ½ tablespoon sesame oil
- 1.5 tablespoon ketchup
- 2 tablespoon brown sugar
- 1 tablespoon soy sauce
- 1 tablespoon gochujang
- 2 tablespoon honey

Garnish (Optional)

- Green onion (sliced)
- Sesame seeds

Method:

1. Add the chicken wings to a pan. Whisk rice wine.
2. Lift the fluid of the wings slowly and put it in a clean bowl.
3. Insert the garlic powder, onion powder, pepper, salt, and ginger powder.
4. Sprinkle some olive oil on the basket of an air fryer.
5. Set the fryer's heat to 400 F and cook.
6. Just remember that, based on the air fryer, the cooking time can vary.
7. Reading the directions below, consider your options of chicken wing sauce.
8. Mix all the sauce ingredients in a small saucepan.

9. Take it to a simmer over medium-high heat, stirring regularly.
10. Mix the corn starch and the boiling water in a jar.
11. Remove from heat and cool it down for three to five minutes until the mixture thickens or changes to glaze.
12. Combine all the sauce ingredients in a small saucepan. Take it to a boil on medium-high heat, stirring regularly.
13. On a covered sheet pan, put the air-fried chicken on it.
14. Cover the chicken softly using a braising brush with your selection of sauce.

3.15 Kimchi Buchimgae

Cooking Time: 25 minutes
Serving Size: 3

Ingredients:
- Some vegetable cooking oil
- dipping sauce to taste
- 2 ½ cups all-purpose flour
- 2 green chili
- 1 red chili
- 2 ½ cups water

- 1 tablespoon Kimchi liquid
- 5 ice cubes
- ½ teaspoon fine sea salt
- 1 large egg (beaten)
- 2 cups Kimchi

Method:

1. Create the batter for the pancake as follows. Filter the salts and the starch.
2. Insert water and swirl well with it. Mix the egg mixture, kimchi, fluid kimchi, and chilies.
3. When well cooked, heat the oil in a pan. Place into the pan a thick layer of cooking oil.
4. Ensure that the oil is distributed over the pan all the way.
5. With a ladle, spoon out the pancake combination and dump it on the bowl. Please ensure it is spread equally.
6. Initially, cook the combination for 20 seconds at medium temperature and then turn the heat down to medium to moderate.
7. When seventy percent of the pancake is fried, flip the pancake over.
8. To keep it moist, press the pancake with the spoon a few times.
9. Cut it into an easy-to-bite size if both surfaces are fried. Serve hot.

3.16 Korean BBQ Beef Ribs

Cooking Time: 8 hours 5 minutes
Serving Size: 4

Ingredients:

- 2 kg beef spare ribs

Marinade

- 2 teaspoon (minced) ginger
- ¼ teaspoon ground black pepper
- ¾ cup soy sauce
- 1 onion
- 2 tablespoon (minced) garlic
- ¼ cup of rice wine
- 1 red apple
- 6 tablespoon brown sugar

Method:

1. Pour the beef over the marinade and ensure it hits all sections of the meat. Wrap the meat, then move it to the refrigerator.
2. Marinate the meat for at least three hours.
3. Preheat the oven to 212F for 20 minutes on an induced fan situation. Lay down a baking tray with some waxed baking parchment or aluminum foil.
4. Then put a marinated rack of ribs in position. Spill the ribs with some marinade, but remove most of the gravy. For eight hours, cook it.
5. Remove the meat and cut it out. Serve hot.

3.17 Sangchu Geotjeori

Cooking Time: 30 minutes
Serving Size: 2

Ingredients:

- 2 green onion (thinly sliced)
- Toasted sesame seeds
- ¼ medium onion (thinly sliced)
- 1 green leaf lettuce

Dressing

- 1 teaspoon sesame seed oil
- ½ teaspoon Gochugaru
- 1½ tablespoons sugar
- 1 tablespoon apple vinegar
- 1½ tablespoons soy sauce
- 2 garlic cloves minced

Method:

1. Clean, rinse, and dry the lettuce.
2. Strips should be 1 inch thick. In a big mixing bowl, combine all of the ingredients.
3. Toss in the spring onion and cabbage.
4. Mix all dressing ingredients in a bowl pan.
5. Mix until the sugar is fully dissolved.
6. Place half of the seasoning over the salad when ready to eat.
7. Toss and taste, adding more dressing if necessary.
8. Sesame seeds can be sprinkled on top. Serve right away.

Chapter 4: Korean Dinner and Desserts Recipes

4.1 Chapssal Donuts

Cooking Time: 55 minutes

Serving Size: 25 donuts

> **Ingredients:**
>
> **Dough**
> - ¼ teaspoon fine sea salt
> - 2 cups hot water
> - 80g self-rising flour
> - 20g melted butter
> - 500g sweet rice flour
>
> **Stuffing**
> - 180g sweetened red bean paste
> - ¼ teaspoon cinnamon powder
>
> **Others**
> - 30g castor sugar
> - Some vegetable oil

Method:
1. In a small mixing bowl, combine the stuffing components.
2. In a big mixing bowl, combine the sweet corn starch and self-rising powder.
3. Combine the salt, warm oil, and hot water in a mixing bowl.

4. To produce mini circular balls, turn the dough out onto a baking sheet and break it into smaller sections.
5. By pushing the formed balls with your hands, you can open up some dough. Open the dough and insert the filling combination.
6. In a small deep saucepan, shallow fry the donut till the dough is lightly browned.
7. Cool for five to ten minutes after placing the cooking doughnuts on a sheet of oil-absorbing paper.
8. Toss the donuts in syrup or roll them in sugar on a tray.
9. Conversely, you might place the sugar in a trash container and then add the donuts.

4.2 Bulgogi Beef Recipe

Cooking Time: 1 hour 15 minutes

Serving Size: 4

Ingredients:

- 2 tablespoons sesame oil
- ½ teaspoon black pepper
- 2 tablespoons garlic
- 2 tablespoons sesame seeds
- 1 pound flank steak
- 2 ½ tablespoons white sugar
- ¼ cup green onion
- 5 tablespoons soy sauce

Method:

1. In a shallow bowl, position the beef. In a small cup, mix the sesame oil, sugar, spring onions, cloves, sesame seeds, soy sauce, salt, and pepper.
2. Pour the sauce over the meat.
3. Put it in the fridge for at least 1 hour or night, covered.
4. Preheat an oven broiler to high heat and brush the grate gently with oil.
5. 1–2 minutes each side on a hot pan, grill meat until lightly seared and cooked through.

4.3 Sweet Rice Bundt Cake

Cooking Time: 50 minutes

Serving Size: 6

Ingredients:

Dry Mixture

- 1 teaspoon fine sea salt
- 1 teaspoon baking powder
- 1 cup brown sweet rice flour
- ½ cup of sugar
- 1 cup sweet rice flour

Wet Mixture

- ½ cup sweet red bean paste
- 1 teaspoon vanilla extract
- 2 oz. unsalted butter (melted)
- 2 each egg

- 1 cup whole milk

Method:

1. Heat the oven to 180C (350F).
2. In the Grinder, process sweet rice and brown rice in the best setting.
3. Melt butter till it becomes completely liquid in the microwave.
4. To avoid sticking, brush or spray Mini Bundt Cake Plate or Cakelette Pan with oil.
5. Add both the sweet brown rice and sweet rice flour to a big mixing pan.
6. Transfer salt and baking soda. With a brush, mix the dry powder.
7. In dry ingredients of six, add the milk, vanilla essence, eggs, sugar, and butter.
8. When using a cake maker, mix until well combined with no lumps, for 2 minutes or more.
9. In the mixture, add in the red bean paste.
10. Pour mixture into cake molds once red bean mixture is uniformly mixed in.
11. Bake thirty minutes for the mini-bundt cake pans.

4.4 Korean Fried Chicken

Cooking Time: 40 minutes

Serving Size: 6

Ingredients:

- ¼ teaspoon ginger powder
- Ground black pepper
- 900g chicken thigh fillets
- 1 teaspoon garlic powder
- 1 teaspoon fine sea salt
- 1 teaspoon onion powder
- 2 tablespoon rice wine

Other

- cooking oil
- 1.5 cups of corn starch

Soy Garlic Sauce

- 2 tablespoon water
- 2 green onions (optional)
- ¼ cups soy sauce
- Ground black pepper
- 3 dried chilies (optional)
- ½ tablespoon (minced) garlic
- 2 tablespoon brown sugar
- 2 tablespoon rice wine
- ½ tablespoon (minced) ginger
- 2 tablespoon honey

Slurry

- 2 teaspoon water
- 2 teaspoon corn starch

Garnish

- green onions (sliced)
- toasted sesame seeds

Method:

1. Put the minced chicken in a wide bowl and whisk in the rice wine, garlic powder, onion, seasoning powder, salt, and pepper.
2. In a wide bowl, put the corn starch in it. In the corn starch, add the seasoned chicken parts and cover them uniformly.
3. Add a reasonable amount of oil to a large skillet (or fryer) and warm it until the oil temperature exceeds 347 F.
4. Add additional chicken thoroughly and fry it until it cooks.
5. Mix all the sauce ingredients in a small saucepan. Carry it to a boil over medium-high heat, stirring regularly.
6. Pull out the chilies and green bits of onion until the sauce begins to bubble.
7. Turn off the heat and cool longer than 5 minutes until the mixture thickens or changes to glaze.
8. On the rimmed baking sheet, position the double-fried chicken.
9. Garnish with sesame seeds and spring onions until all the chicken is covered with the sauce.

4.5 Korean Walnut Pastry

Cooking Time: 30 minutes

Serving Size: 30

Ingredients:

Batter
- 1 tablespoon melted butter
- 1 egg
- 1 cup cake flour (sifted)
- 1 cup water or milk
- 3 tablespoon castor sugar (raw)
- 2 teaspoon baking powder (sifted)
- ¼ teaspoon fine sea salt

Filling
- 15 walnuts (shelled)
- 200g (sweetened) red bean paste

Others
- 1 tablespoon melted butter

Method:
1. Mix all batter components in a medium-scale pan.
2. Brush the two sides of the pot with some butter or olive oil rapidly.
3. Pour the mixture of the batter onto the walnut cake tray.
4. To coat the walnut cake base, apply the red bean mixture and walnuts, and then add further batter sauce on top.
5. Heat both edges of the skillet until it turns light golden on the walnut cake.
6. To avoid burning the cake, remember to check the crispiness of the cake fairly frequently.
7. Take the pastry from the skillet and quickly cool down on a shelf.

8. Repeat the steps before all the ingredients are used.

4.6 Makgeolli Ice Cream

Cooking Time: 30 minutes

Serving Size: 6

Ingredients:

- 2 tablespoon lemon juice
- 2 tablespoon walnuts (chopped)
- 230ml makgeolli
- 1 tablespoon corn starch
- ¼ teaspoon of sea salt
- 200ml heavy whipping cream
- 100g sugar
- 150ml whole milk

Method:

1. Combine makgeolli and sugar into a small pot.
2. Bring to the boil, and then on medium heat, simmer until one half is decreased.
3. Combine the corn starch with 50ml of milk. Just set aside.
4. Transfer 130 ml of makgeolli into another big saucepan.
5. Once the syrup and makgeolli condense are chilled, add milk, makgeolli mixture.
6. Mix the cornstarch and milk combination once more when boiling, then return the cornstarch and milk combination to the bowl.
7. Continue whisking until the stuff thickens.

8. Up to end, add some salt, combine and let it cool. Toss the heavy cream till you get a soft top when the ice cream base has settled.

9. Sliced nuts are optionally included in this phase to create nutty ice cream.

4.7 Nut-Free Energy Balls

Cooking Time: 15 minutes

Serving Size: 28

Ingredients:

- 2 tablespoon coconut oil
- 2 tablespoon water
- 2 cups pitted dates
- ¼ cup raw cacao powder
- 1 tablespoon chia seeds
- 1 cup fine desiccated coconut

Method:

1. In a mixing bowl, mix all ingredients and process them once creamy and well combined (15 - 20 seconds).
2. In a stand mixer, pass the combined ingredients.
3. Squeeze out the cooked ingredients equal to one tablespoon. To form it into a sphere, roll it around your hand.
4. Set it aside until done. With the rest of the ingredients, replicate this.
5. Serve cold.

4.8 Korean Steak, Kimchi, and Cauliflower Rice Bowls

Cooking Time: 30 minutes

Serving Size: 4

Ingredients:

- ½ cup kimchi
- 1-ounce radishes
- 2 tablespoons sesame seeds
- 1 cup carrots
- 2 large eggs
- 1 pound sirloin steak
- ¼ cup gochujang
- 4 tablespoons sesame oil
- 1 tablespoon ginger
- ¼ teaspoon salt
- 2 scallions
- 6 cups riced cauliflower

Method:

1. Over high heat, carry a large bowl of water on the stove.
2. Place an ice water bowl by the burner.
3. Allow five minutes for the whites to cool in the ice bucket.
4. In a medium saucepan, heat 2 tablespoons of oil over moderate flame.
5. Combine the cauliflower, spring onion whites, spice, and salt in a large mixing bowl. Cook for approximately 5 minutes.
6. In the same pan, heat and cook 2 tablespoons of oil on moderate flame.
7. Cook, occasionally stirring, until the steak is no longer pink, two to four minutes.

8. Split the cauliflower into four bowls to combine.

4.9 Chapssaltteok

Cooking Time: 24 minutes

Serving Size: 6

Ingredients:

- ¾ cup (sweetened) red bean paste (shape round)
- 3 tablespoon corn starch
- ¾ cup sweet rice flour
- A pinch fine sea salt
- ½ cup of water
- ¼ cup castor sugar

Method:

1. In a microwave-proof medium bowl, mix the sweet rice flour, salt, and sugar.
2. Fill a bowl with cling wrap, leaving a slight opening to escape from the steam.
3. Put the cup, covering again in the microwave, and heat it for another two minutes.
4. From the microwave, take the bowl.
5. Spread the corn starch gently on the surface.
6. Detach the mochi paste from the mixture carefully and put it on the board. Then, break the roll into six bits using a scraper.
7. Deflate softly and expand the dough on your hand, and position the red bean paste balls in the center.
8. By collecting the edges of the dough, cover the rice cake.

9. With the rest of the ingredients, replicate this step. Serve at ambient temperature.

4.10 Hodduk (Korean Sweet Pancakes)

Cooking Time: 1 hour 50 minutes
Serving Size: 6

Ingredients:
- ½ cup lukewarm milk
- Some cooking oil
- 1 teaspoon white sugar
- 1 teaspoon instant dry yeast
- ½ teaspoon fine sea salt
- 1 ¼ cup all-purpose flour

Fillings
- ¼ teaspoon cinnamon powder
- 2 tablespoon nuts
- ¼ cup dark brown sugar

Method:
1. In a big mixing bowl, sieve the wheat, then add salt, glucose, fermentation, and milk.
2. If the flour has been lifted, hit it a few times with your palms to release pressure. Stop for the next 20 minutes, covered with the sheet.
3. Place one of the dough parts in your hands and straighten it with your palms so that you can insert about one tablespoon of stuffing.
4. A frying pan should be preheated on moderate flame.

5. Switch it over and use a sturdy turner or a skilled hotteok pump to press the dough flat. Cook till lightly browned on the sides
6. Place the pancake on a sheet and repeat with the leftover dough. Enjoy while it is still warm!

4.11 Dalgona - Korean Sugar Sponge Candy

Cooking Time: 8 minutes

Serving Size: 1

Ingredients:

- 1 teaspoon vegetable oil
- 1 pinch baking soda
- 1 tablespoon sugar

Method:

1. Use a little vegetable oil to cover a plate or a steel or ground surface.
2. In a spatula or large spoon, apply two tablespoons of sugar.
3. At medium-high heat, keep the spoon or spatula on top of the stove and melt the sugar for around 3-5 minutes.
4. When it melts, avoid burning by continually moving with a spoon and remove it from the heat if it begins to smoke.
5. Remove the spoon from the heat instantly and combine the soda with the syrup.
6. Back at the top of the heat, shift the ladle just once and reheat for just about 4-5 seconds.
7. Move the mixture of sugar and beverage to a lubricated plate or board.

8. Push for three seconds or so, and then force your mold on the candy.
9. Chill in the refrigerator and serve.

4.12 Bungeoppang with Filling

Cooking Time: 30 minutes
Serving Size: 4

Ingredients:
- 9 tablespoon milk
- ¼ teaspoon pinch of salt
- 75g all-purpose flour
- ½ teaspoon baking powder
- 1 egg
- 35g sweet rice flour (mochiko)
- ½ teaspoon baking soda

For Filling
- 200g (canned) sweet red beans
- 1 tablespoon melted butter

Method:
1. Stir all of the dry ingredients.
2. In a dish, combine the egg and milk apart.
3. Combine the dry and wet components thoroughly.
4. Lower heat to medium and just around ¼ pour all batter into one portion of the molds (2 fishes). That is enough to cover a fish's eye.
5. Spoon the red beans into the middle of the fish quickly.

6. To completely cover the half-fish mold, add batter on the tops of the red beans.
7. Immediately close the pot and turn it over.
8. Bring the heat up to medium-low, a little above.
9. Cook for an additional 2:30 minutes on each hand.
10. After two minutes, you can open it to check the density. If it is not brown yet, heat more.
11. On both sides, if brown, move to a plate and leave to cool for a few minutes.
12. The red bean stuffing can be Very Warm, so be careful and cautious.

4.13 Korean Shaved Ice Dessert

Cooking Time: 8 minutes

Serving Size: 2

Ingredients:

- 6 strawberries (sliced)
- ½ cup blueberries
- Ice shaver machine and ice
- 2 tablespoon misugaru
- 3 tablespoon mini mochi rice cake
- ½ cup sweet red beans
- 2 tablespoon (sweetened) condensed milk

Method:
1. If a specific round icebox is used, fill it with water and place it in the refrigerator to make ice.

2. Some devices will even let you produce shaved ice from normal ice cubes.
3. Cut strawberries into pieces.
4. Shave the ice into a jar that is wide enough to accommodate it all.
5. Insert the berries and a small cake of mochi.
6. Top or sides with a spoon of soft red beans and then glaze with condensed milk.

4.14 Baram Tteok

Cooking Time: 25 minutes

Serving Size: 16 balls

Ingredients:
- Red food coloring
- Some cornstarch
- 1½ cup red bean paste
- Green food coloring
- 2 cups glutinous rice
- 7 tablespoons sugar
- 1 cup water
- 1 teaspoon salt

Method:
1. Combine the glutinous corn starch, salt, spice, and food coloring in a mixing bowl.
2. Slowly drizzle in the water, constantly stirring until all of the components are thoroughly combined.
3. Cover with a piece of plastic wrap. Microwave for five minutes on high or until finished.

4. Re-knead the dough for at least a few minutes.
5. Ping-pong-ball-sized red bean paste is divided into six to twelve balls.
6. Make two long cylinders out of the dough.
7. Put the ball of bean in the center of a flattened piece.
8. Place the rice dough around the ball.
9. Efficiently roll the ball. Cornstarch should be used to coat the surface.

4.15 Korean Coffee Brownies

Cooking Time: 35 minutes

Serving Size: 12

Ingredients:
- 1 cup all-purpose flour
- 2 tablespoons cocoa powder
- ¼ teaspoon kosher salt
- 2 large eggs
- 110g unsalted butter
- 1½ cups sugar
- 1 tablespoon vanilla extract
- Korean instant coffee 36g
- 110g chocolate

Method:
1. Set the oven to 175 degrees Celsius.
2. Warm the oil, cocoa, and espresso in the top of the double cooker over low heat, swirling periodically.

3. Continue to beat in the whites with the teaspoon or slotted spoon, pounding well after each inclusion.
4. Work in the flour and cocoa powder for one minute.
5. Soft the top of the mixture into the ready baking pan.
6. Place the pan on a cooling rack fully, around 45 minutes. Trim the pan's sides with a small knife.
7. Move to a baking sheet and, using a paring blade, slice into 2-inch squares.

4.16 Bingsu with Sweet Red Beans

Cooking Time: 8 minutes

Serving Size: 2

Ingredients:
- 6 strawberries (sliced)
- ½ cup blueberries
- Ice shaver machine and ice
- 2 tablespoon misugaru
- 3 tablespoon mini mochi rice cake
- ½ cup sweet red beans
- 2 tablespoon (sweetened) condensed milk

Method:
1. Remove the cans bag and wash the berries, and prepare the assembling of each topping.
2. Cut strawberries into pieces.

3. Shave the ice into a jar that is wide enough to accommodate it all.
4. It is unnecessary to arrange toppings but to cover ice uniformly, you might want to use a small strainer to sprinkle the misugaru on ice.
5. Insert the berries and a small cake of mochi. Top or sides with a spoon of soft red beans and then glaze with condensed milk.

4.17 Paleo Songpyeon

Cooking Time: 12 minutes
Serving Size: 20

Ingredients:

Songpyeon Wrapper

- 2 large eggs
- 1 tablespoon rice vinegar
- ¼ cup tapioca starch
- ⅛ teaspoon sea salt
- ½ cup blanched almond flour
- 1¼ cup cassava flour

For Pink Dough

- 1 tablespoon coconut sugar
- ⅛ teaspoon sea salt
- ½ cup toasted sesame seeds
- 2 tablespoon honey
- 2 tablespoon pureed beets
- Sweet sesame filling
- Water as needed

For Green Dough
- Water as needed
- 4 teaspoon matcha powder

For Yellow Dough
- Water as needed
- 2 teaspoon turmeric powder

Other ingredients
- Sesame oil
- Coldwater

Method:
1. To create the wrapping dough, combine all of the components in a mixing bowl and mix with a fork till crumbly.
2. While thawing, add 1 tablespoon of extra water till the texture resembles playdough and it can be easily molded.
3. In a mixing bowl, mix all of the filling components.
4. Take the dough out of the freezer. Form the dough into a ball.
5. A steamer basket should be placed on top of 1 gallon of water in a pot.
6. Over medium heat, carry the mixture to a boil. Fill the steamer basket halfway with songpyeon.
7. Drain well, then mix with a healthy portion of sesame oil.

Chapter 5: Vegetarian Korean Recipes

5.1 Vegan Bibimbap

Cooking Time: 70 minutes
Serving Size: 4

Ingredients:

- Fried egg, (optional)
- Gochujang (red pepper paste)
- 2 cups of Korean rice
- 2 teaspoons salt (divided)
- ½ pound meat (optional)
- 1 zucchini (sliced)
- 2 tablespoons sesame oil (divided)
- 1 large cucumber (sliced)
- 1 ½ cups bean sprouts
- 2 carrots (julienned)
- 4 shiitake mushrooms
- 1 ½ cups spinach
- Dash of sesame seeds

Method:
1. Collect ingredients.
2. In addition, this will change the taste.
3. On the stove, prepare rice.
4. In saltwater, add cucumber pieces.

5. Then, put two teaspoons of sesame oil, 1 dash of salt, and a splash of sesame seeds into the spinach.
6. Spinach gets flavored with sesame seed, pepper, and sesame oil.
7. After that, you will have to sauté the carrots with a sprinkle of salt.
8. Next, give a touch of salt to the mushrooms.
9. Sauté the zucchini with a sprinkle of salt after that.
10. Beef, eggs, or even both can be positioned in the center if required.
11. To eat, transfer to your dish a bit of oil and the required amount of gochujang, and combine it all with a fork.

5.2 Mushroom Hot Pot

Cooking Time: 30 minutes

Serving Size: 2

Ingredients:
Vegetable Broth

- 1 tablespoon soup soy sauce
- Salt and pepper to taste
- ½ small onion
- A few mushroom stems
- 3 ounces Korean radish

Vegetables

- 10 ounces mushrooms
- 2 scallions
- 2 ounces watercress
- ½ teaspoon (minced) garlic

Method:

1. In a small saucepan, put five cups of water and the soup veggies.
2. Carry it over medium temperature to a boil.
3. Turn the heat down to moderate and simmer for fifteen minutes or so. Throw the veggie's waste.
4. Season with salt, soft soy sauce, and black pepper.
5. Break the mushrooms into bite-size pieces. Cook the mushrooms a little bit, so do not cut them too small.

6. Split longitudinally into bite-size parts when using oyster mushrooms.

7. Organize the mushrooms and green onions carefully in a deep pot in clusters.

8. Boil until the mushrooms are tender, for four to five minutes, over moderate to medium-high heat.

9. When you are preparing at the table, you can include more soup and any leftover vegetables before dining.

5.3 Vegan Tteokbokki

Cooking Time: 15 minutes

Serving Size: 2

Ingredients:

- 3 scallions
- Toasted sesame seeds
- 1 tablespoon granulated sugar
- 10 tubular rice cakes
- ¼ cup gochujang paste
- ½ tablespoon Korean red pepper flakes
- 2 cups of vegetable broth

Method:

1. In a pan, carry vegetable broth to heat.
2. Add the gochujang, red pepper, and sugar syrup once the broth has reached a simmer.
3. Stir carefully, then gently fold in the rice cakes.
4. Reduce the heat to mild and top with 1/3 of the green onion.

5. Cook, occasionally stirring, for 7-10 minutes, just until the liquid is thick and glossy. Every few moments, give it a gentle stir.
6. Ladle into a cup and top with the remaining green onion and sesame seeds to serve.

5.4 Zucchini Pancakes

Cooking Time: 45 minutes

Serving Size: 4

Ingredients:
- 1 large egg
- vegetable oil for frying
- 1 zucchini
- 2 green chili peppers (sliced)
- ½ cup buchim garu
- ¼ sweet onion (sliced)
- ½ teaspoon salt
- Dipping Sauce
- pinch of black pepper
- pinch gochugaru
- 1 tablespoon soy sauce
- 1 tablespoon water
- ½ teaspoon sugar
- 1 teaspoon vinegar

Method:
1. The zucchini should be cut into long thin pieces. In a cup, put them and spray with ½ teaspoon salt.

2. Let stay for approximately ten minutes until some liquid is simmered and emitted.
3. Squeeze as much of the fluid as necessary out of the zucchini and reserve the liquid in the cup. Put down the zucchini.
4. Transfer the egg and pancake mixture.
5. When stirring, the zucchini mixture will look rigid, and after a few moments, this will become more fluid.
6. Over moderate flame, heat a pan with two tablespoons of olive oil.
7. In a thin round form, add about two sprinkling tablespoons of the mixture and distribute it uniformly.
8. Reduce the heat to moderate and simmer until light lightly browned on the bottom, around two minutes on each side. Serve with side dishes.

5.5 Braised Potatoes

Cooking Time: 30 minutes

Serving Size: 4

Ingredients:

- ¼ onion
- 1 tablespoon cooking oil
- 1.5 pounds of potatoes
- 3 green chili peppers
- 1 carrot

Braising Liquid

- 1 teaspoon sesame oil
- ½ teaspoon roasted sesame seeds

- 3 tablespoons soy sauce
- pinch black pepper
- ¾ cup of water
- 1 tablespoon sugar
- 1 tablespoon corn syrup
- 1 teaspoon (minced) garlic
- 1 tablespoon rice wine

Method:
1. Slice and cut the potatoes into pieces of approximately 1 inch. In large chunks, cut the onion, carrots, and pepper.
2. Sauté the potato in olive oil in a non-stick skillet over medium-high heat for 4 - 5 minutes, stirring regularly so that the potatoes do not bind to the pot.
3. Apply the mixture of sauce and bring to a simmer over medium temperature.
4. Drop pieces of carrot in.
5. Cover and turn the heat down to moderate and cook till the potatoes are almost ready.
6. Mix in the onions and green peppers and simmer for about three minutes.
7. Mix in the sesame oil and apply the sesame seeds to the mixture. Serve hot.

5.6 Korean White Radish Kimchi

Cooking Time: 48 hours 15 minutes

Serving Size: 12

Ingredients:

- 4 green onions (sliced)
- 10 cups of water
- 8 medium Korean radishes
- 4 tablespoon sugar
- 4 cloves of garlic (sliced)
- 6 tablespoon of sea salt

Method:

1. With 3 tablespoons of salt and two tablespoons of sugar, coat the radishes. Let it remain at room temperature for one day.
2. Dissolve three tablespoons of salt and two tablespoons of sugar into hot water after one day.
3. For salted radishes, cloves, and scallions, add water.
4. Store in the refrigerator when the broth has reached a sour, vinegary taste.
5. Put vegetables and a thick layer of broth in a bowl or wide cup to serve.

5.7 Mushroom Bulgogi Lettuce Wraps

Cooking Time: 1 hour

Serving Size: 6

Ingredients:

- 2 heads butter lettuce
- 4 cups cooked brown rice

- ½ cup low-sodium soy sauce
- 3 pounds assorted cremini and button mushrooms (quartered)
- 4 scallions (sliced)
- 4 tablespoons canola oil (divided)
- 1 yellow onion (sliced)
- 2 ½ tablespoons dark brown sugar
- 2 tablespoons of rice wine vinegar
- 4 teaspoons toasted sesame oil
- 6 garlic cloves (minced)
- 2 tablespoons (minced) ginger

Optional

- toasted sesame seeds
- Lime wedges
- 2 Persian cucumbers (sliced)
- Kimchee
- Korean hot pepper paste
- 2 jalapeños (sliced)

Method:

1. In non-reactive containers, mix with soy sauce, brown sugar, ginger, garlic, rice wine vinegar, and sesame oil and set it aside once ready for use.
2. Heat one tablespoon of olive oil over moderate heat in a large deep fryer.
3. Add the onion as the oil glitters, and wisps of smoke fall off the edge. Cook for about three minutes.

4. Cover and transfer the pan to the stove in a large bowl.
5. Add three tablespoons of oil and add one-third of the mushrooms to the mixture.
6. Cook, stirring periodically, around eight minutes.
7. To cook off any leftover mushrooms, add mushrooms to the onion mixture and repeat several times more.
8. In the meantime, in a medium bowl, put half of the marinade and cook over medium-high heat till reduced significantly around four minutes.
9. Cook until marinated, around five minutes, and the mushrooms are coated with a light coating.
10. Remove from flame, add decreased green onion and marinade and mix through.

5.8 Crunchy Gochujang Cauliflower

Cooking Time: 50 minutes

Serving Size: 2

Ingredients:
- ½ tablespoon sesame oil
- 1 tablespoon sesame seeds
- 2 whole scallions
- 1/3 cup vegetable broth
- 2 leaves red cabbage

- 1 carrot
- 1 head cauliflower
- ¼ cup onion
- 6 cloves garlic
- 1 tablespoon vegetable base
- 4 cups vegetable oil
- 1 tablespoon olive oil
- 3 tablespoons plant milk
- 1 teaspoon vegetarian oyster sauce
- 1 teaspoon mustard
- 1 tablespoon soy sauce
- 1 tablespoon light soy sauce
- 1 teaspoon gochujang
- 1 tablespoon garlic powder
- 1 teaspoon black pepper
- 2 tablespoons maple syrup
- 2 cups corn starch

Method:
1. In a big mixing bowl, combine the cauliflower pieces.
2. Add 1 cup corn starch, ½ tablespoon garlic paste, and ½ teaspoon cayenne pepper in another big mixing bowl.
3. Whisk together the sauce ingredients ahead of time.
4. Preheat the vegetable oil to 350°F in a big cast-iron skillet or frying pan.

5. Cook your cauliflower for five minutes, just until the sides start to brown.
6. Continue cooking and add onion, cabbage, carrot, and green onions to the pan once the oil is warmed.
7. Heat for another thirty seconds after adding the vegetable broth.
8. Spray the sesame oil on top after drizzling them with soy sauce. Serve right away.

5.9 Korean Vegan Kimchi

Cooking Time: 1 hour

Serving Size: 16

Ingredients:
- 3 scallions
- 3 large mustard green
- 1 large Napa cabbage
- 5 cups of water
- ¾ pound Korean radish
- 1 cup Korean coarse sea salt

Seasonings
- 2 tablespoons salt
- 1 cup dashima (dried)
- 1 tablespoon sweet rice powder
- 1 teaspoon (grated) ginger
- 2 tablespoons soup soy sauce
- ½ cup Korean red pepper flakes
- ½ cup pumpkin puree

- 2 tablespoons (minced) garlic
- ¼ Korean pear (grated)

Method:

1. Lengthwise, slice the side of the stem of the cabbage in the quarter, just around three to four inches in.
2. Dissolve half of a cup of salt in five cups of water in a wide pan.
3. Drizzle salt evenly over each leaf's thick white portion.
4. Try salting all the cabbage pieces with a half teaspoon of salt.
5. In the meantime, make the rice mixture and the broth and cool.
6. Combine all the ingredients with the seasoning.
7. Slice the green onion finely and the other mustard green.
8. In the jar with the radish mixture, position one cabbage half.
9. With ¼ cup of broth, wash the bowl containing the radish mixture and spill over the kimchi.

5.10 Quick Korean Spicy Slaw Recipe

Cooking Time: 35 minutes

Serving Size: 4

Ingredients:

- 1 tablespoon soy sauce
- 2 tablespoons sesame seeds
- 1 Napa cabbage (sliced)

- 2 cloves garlic (pressed)
- 1 tablespoon (grated) fresh ginger
- 3 tablespoons Korean chile paste
- 2 tablespoons grapeseed oil
- 1 cup red cabbage (sliced)
- 4 green onions (chopped)
- 1 red bell pepper (seeded and sliced)
- 6 tablespoons rice vinegar
- 1 large carrot (shredded)

Method:
1. In a big bowl, put the cabbage, spring onions, carrots, and red bell pepper.
2. Transfer the rice vinegar, oil, gochujang, ginger, seasoning, and soy sauce to a glass jar installed with a lid.
3. Move or swirl if it does not integrate very well, pour over the combination of cabbage.
4. Toss to cover with sesame oil and edge. Chill in the fridge for up to fifteen minutes.

5.11 Watermelon Kimchi

Cooking Time: 1 day 30 minutes

Serving Size: 4

Ingredients:

- ¼ cup (minced) red onion
- Toasted sesame seeds
- 1 ½ pound watermelon rind
- 1 tablespoon red pepper flakes

- 5 scallions (sliced)
- 2 tablespoons (chopped) fresh ginger
- 2 tablespoons gochujang paste
- 2 tablespoons kosher salt
- 2 tablespoons sugar
- 6 cloves garlic (chopped)
- ¼ cup of fish sauce

Method:
1. Cut the watermelon rind into 2 inches parts or slice the rind into very thin slices using a sharp knife.
2. Spray with the salts and put the thin watermelon strips in a strainer. Toss well, then let it stay for about thirty minutes to drain.
3. In the meantime, in a mixing bowl, put the fish sauce, sugar, ginger, garlic, and gochujang paste and combine to mix.
4. In a large mixing bowl, put the paste and mix the chili flakes, green onions, and red onion.
5. With ice water, wash the watermelon rind, then compress it into handfuls to extract excess water.
6. On a fresh, clean dishtowel, stretch out the watermelon rind with the rind inside it.
7. Unwrap the dishtowel and insert the marinade with the watermelon rind. To mix, flip.
8. When serving, move the kimchi to a clean container, seal, chill in the fridge, and let marinate for at least 24 hours.

5.12 Classic Korean Bibimbap

Cooking Time: 70 minutes

Serving Size: 4

Ingredients:
- Fried egg, (optional)
- Gochujang (red pepper paste)
- 2 cups of Korean rice
- 2 teaspoons salt (divided)
- ½ pound meat (optional)
- 1 zucchini (sliced)
- 2 tablespoons sesame oil (divided)
- 1 large cucumber (sliced)
- 1 ½ cups bean sprouts
- 2 carrots (julienned)
- 4 shiitake mushrooms
- 1 ½ cups spinach
- Dash of sesame seeds

Method:
1. On the stove, prepare rice.
2. In saltwater, add cucumber pieces. Then use a strainer, clean the cucumber strips.
3. Then, put two teaspoons of sesame oil, 1 dash of salt, and a splash of sesame seeds into the spinach.
4. Spinach gets flavored with sesame seed, pepper, and sesame oil.

5. Use two tablespoons of sesame oil and a dash of sesame seeds to season the bean sprouts.
6. Next, give a touch of salt to the mushrooms.
7. Sauté the zucchini with a sprinkle of salt after that.
8. Then in a large mixing bowl, place the rice and organize the veggies on it.
9. To eat, transfer to your dish a bit of oil and the required amount of gochujang, and combine it all with a fork.

5.13 Korean Soft Tofu Stew

Cooking Time: 1 hour 10 minutes

Serving Size: 4

Ingredients:

- 2 eggs
- 1 scallion (diced)
- 10 anchovies
- 2 teaspoons sesame oil
- 1 package (silken tofu)
- 1 teaspoon sugar
- 4 tablespoons Korean chili flakes
- ⅓ of a daikon radish
- 1 cup kimchi

- 2 teaspoons salt
- 1 small onion (sliced)
- 1 cup pork belly
- 1 piece (dried) kelp
- 3 shiitake mushrooms (dried)
- 1 tablespoon canola oil (divided)
- 2 cloves garlic (minced)
- 5 cups of water

Method:
1. Prepare the anchovy stock first.
2. Add five cups of water in a small saucepan with the chopped anchovies, radish pieces, kelp, and shiitake mushrooms.
3. Put it to a boil with water. Simmer for 25 minutes.
4. Strain the stock after 25 minutes. Save it and slice the mushrooms thinly.
5. Heat a small container or your stew pot over medium-high heat.
6. Fry till the onions are transparent and stir.
7. Insert about 1 ¼ cups of anchovy stock followed by sugar, salt, Korean chili flakes, and sesame oil.
8. Then, add the tofu, around a quarter of a regular size or half of a line.
9. Lightly break the tofu into large chunks. Over the base of each pan, crack the egg, and cook for one minute.

5.14 Eggplant Rolls

Cooking Time: 1 hour 10 minutes

Serving Size: 4

Ingredients:

- Salt and pepper
- 3 tablespoons of perilla
- 2 Asian eggplants (thick)

Filling Type 1

- 3 ounces of red cabbage (sliced)
- 1 package of sprouts

Soy-Based Sauce

- 1 tablespoon soy sauce
- 1 tablespoon apple juice
- 1 tablespoon vinegar
- 1 teaspoon sugar

Filling Type 2

- ¼ green bell pepper
- 1 package mushrooms
- ¼ red bell pepper
- ¼ yellow bell pepper
- ¼ orange bell pepper

Hot Mustard Sauce

- 2 tablespoon juice from the (grated) pear
- ¼ teaspoon salt
- 2 teaspoons Dijon mustard
- 1 tablespoon rice syrup
- 2 tablespoons vinegar

Method:

1. Arrange the veggies by slicing them finely.
2. By pushing a peeler via the eggplant.
3. To cut even strips that are as large as possible with a slicer.
4. To cut the eggplant, you can also use a hand cutter.
5. With a tablespoon of olive oil, warm a pan. Put the eggplant slices in a thin layer, spray gently with salt and black pepper, and simmer slightly over medium-high heat, and one or two minutes on each side. Move to a dish.
6. On a level surface, place an eggplant piece.
7. Repeat until all the slices of eggplant are being used. Serve hot with rice.

5.15 Korean Spicy Pickled Cabbage

Cooking Time: 30 minutes

Serving Size: 12

Ingredients:

- 5 scallions
- Optional: fish sauce
- 10 cups of water
- ½ cup kochukaru
- 2 tablespoons sugar
- 1 tablespoon garlic (chopped)
- 1 tablespoon ginger (chopped)
- 2 Napa cabbages

- 1 cup coarse salt

Method:
1. Collect all ingredients.
2. Add the salt into the liquid in a big, non-reactive bowl or jar.
3. Add the cabbage to the saltwater and weigh down with a serving platter if necessary. For 6 hours, soak the cabbage.
4. Cover and rinse the cabbage in cold water, squeezing the remaining water out.
5. Combine the garlic, spice, red pepper, sugar, and green onions in a big dish.
6. Add the cabbage and cover with the mixture to season.
7. In a wide airtight jar with a cover, load the seasoned cabbage.

5.16 Chilled Soy Milk Noodle Soup

Cooking Time: 30 minutes

Serving Size: 4

Ingredients:
- 1 small tomato (sliced)
- wheat flour noodles 4 ounces
- 1 cup (dried) soybeans
- 2 teaspoons (roasted) sesame seeds
- 1 cucumber (julienned)
- 4 tablespoons (roasted) pine nuts

Method:

1. For six hours or night, wash and drain one cup of dried soybeans.
2. To chill the beans, drain and put them in ice water. To remove the excess, rub the beans with your fingertips.
3. For a smooth milk-like consistency, pass the puree via a fine strainer, swirling to push it through with a fork.
4. Slightly spiced to your taste. Just stir well. To freeze, put it in the fridge. To a simmer, put a medium pot of boiling water.
5. Somyeon noodles are cooked according to package directions (approximately three minutes).
6. Stir up the solids found on the soy milk base and pour in a mixing bowl over the noodles.
7. Garnish the carrots, tomato bits, and sesame seeds with the julienned ones.

5.17 Tofu Gimbap

Cooking Time: 2 hours

Serving Size: 5

> **Ingredients:**
> - 5 nori sheets
>
> **Rice**
> - salt ½ teaspoon
> - 1 tablespoon sesame oil
> - 2 cups of grain rice
>
> **For the Fillings**
> - salt
> - cooking oil

- 10 ounces firm tofu
- 1 burdock root
- sesame oil
- 1 bunch spinach
- 3 Kirby cucumbers
- 2 medium carrots
- 1 teaspoon sesame oil

Method:
1. Use a little liquid than normal, cook rice.
2. Break the tofu into sticks that are around ¾ inches long. Hold, spray gently with salt, and clean with a clean cloth.
3. To protect the pan, warm a small pan with enough oil. Insert the bits of tofu and cook until they are nicely browned on all sides.
4. Over medium temperature, bring a big pot of water to the boil, and prepare an ice bucket.
5. Place a skillet over medium heat with just a little bit of oil. Cook the cucumber until it softens. Season lightly with salt. Cut the Carrots in Julienne.
6. Heat a skillet over medium heat with just a little bit of oil. Stir and fry the carrots until tender. Season lightly with salt.
7. Place about ¾ cup to one cup of rice uniformly and ideally use a rice paddle or your hands.
8. Then begin to roll again and use both hands, applying pressure equally over the roll.
9. Use the sharp knife with a little bit of sesame oil. This is going to prevent the rice from binding to the knife. Following each cut, repeat as required.

5.18 Korean Street Toast

Cooking Time: 20 minutes

Serving Size: 2

Ingredients:
- 4 slices of ham
- Ketchup
- 4 large eggs
- 4 slices of bread
- 40g cheddar cheese (grated)
- Sea salt
- 100g cabbage (chopped)
- Butter
- Pepper
- 35g carrots (chopped)
- 1 spring onion (chopped)

Method:
1. Add a little salt and peppers and place the eggs in a dish. Mix until well blended.
2. Transfer to the beaten egg the green onions, carrot, and vegetables. Just balance them well.
3. Over medium heat, warm a deep fryer and spread some oil around the skillet, and drop the egg and vegetable mixture in.
4. Try to form a rectangle with the beaten egg. As the eggs warm up, it gets simpler.
5. Break it in two when the omelet is prepared on one side, and turn each one cautiously. Slice them on a plate when they are fried.

6. Use a dishtowel to clean the deep fryer, add a bit more oil, and fry the bread.
7. Place the other piece of toast on top of the tomato sauce to make a sandwich when the toast is roasted on the side. With the leftover slice, repeat.

5.19 Korean Green Salad

Cooking Time: 10 minutes

Serving Size: 3

Ingredients:
- 4 chrysanthemum leaves
- 3 each green onions
- 8 each perilla leaves
- 1 each red leaf lettuce (small)

Soy Dressing
- 1 teaspoon sesame oil
- 1 teaspoon sesame seeds
- 1 teaspoon Korean red chili powder
- 2 tablespoon green onions
- 1 tablespoon rice vinegar
- 1 tablespoon sugar
- 4 teaspoon soy sauce

Method:
1. Greens should be washed and rinsed. Drain the water.
2. When serving entire lettuce bits, slice perilla leaf into 1/3-inch wide strips.

3. Add vegetable oil, vinegar, and syrup until the glucose is fully dissolved to make my Korean seasoning known as Yangnyeom Jang.
4. Combine the rest of the ingredients in a mixing bowl.
5. Mix thoroughly after tossing torn vegetables with Korean soy coating.

5.20 Korean Salad with Sesame Dressing

Cooking Time: 5 minutes

Serving Size: 12

Ingredients:
- 3 tablespoons sesame oil
- 1 tablespoon red chili pepper
- ¼ cup water
- 3 tablespoons rice vinegar
- 2 tablespoons white sugar
- ¼ cup low-sodium soy sauce

Method:
1. In a mixing bowl, combine the soy sauce, salt, liquid, garlic powder, sesame oil, and red chili pepper.
2. Thoroughly combine and serve.

Conclusion

Most of today's Korean food and the customs that accompany it are derived from royal food and the intricate customs of the imperial court. The food is a balanced analysis, with careful attention paid to heat, sweetness, texture, and appearance, as well as thoughtful display. The most important lesson to learn from Korean history is how well they preserved their culture through cooking. Korean temples food still has all of the foods that monks and nuns consumed in ancient times to keep their minds open when training. From 58 BC to 667 AD, the third dynasty brought in several disturbances and institutions that are now the foundation of Goguryeo, advanced Korea. A Korean buffet consists of various dishes that have been steamed, boiled, pan-fried, simmered, preserved, and served fresh. Many spice mixes are selected, preserved, or steamed, and many are hot, as the Koreans have mastered the art of food preservation. Kimchi, Korea's popular spicy cabbage, comes in over a hundred different varieties made with various veggies and is a staple of any meal. It is loved for its sweet, tart texture as well as its ability to help digestion. There is still a lot to speak about in Korea, from its rich past to the amazing variety of healthy meals. Try recipes and enjoy Korean meals at home.

Printed in Great Britain
by Amazon